BEGINNING PIANO SOLO

STAR WARS

ISBN 978-1-4768-7463-0

HAL•LEONARD®
CORPORATION
7777 W. BLUEMOUND RD. P.O. BOX 13819 MILWAUKEE, WI 53213

In Australia Contact:
Hal Leonard Australia Pty. Ltd.
4 Lentara Court
Cheltenham, Victoria, 3192 Australia
Email: ausadmin@halleonard.com.au

Visit Hal Leonard Online at
www.halleonard.com

ACROSS THE STARS

Love Theme from STAR WARS: EPISODE II - ATTACK OF THE CLONES

Music by
JOHN WILLIAMS

Gently

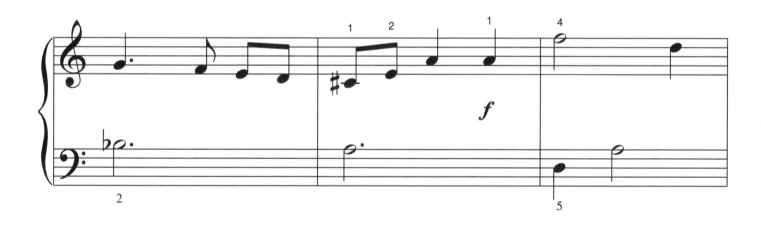

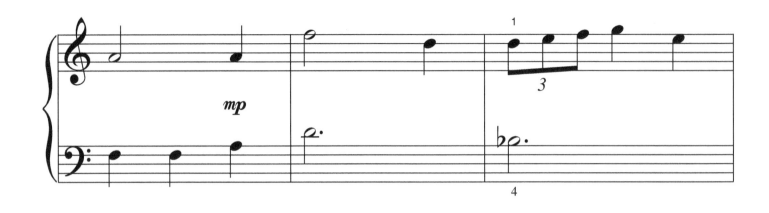

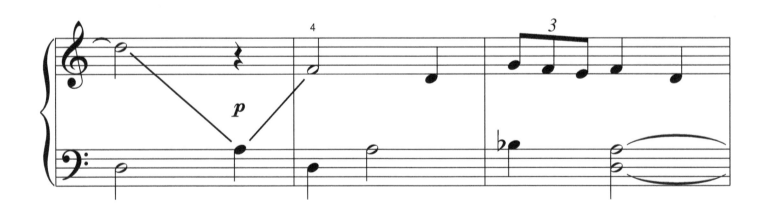

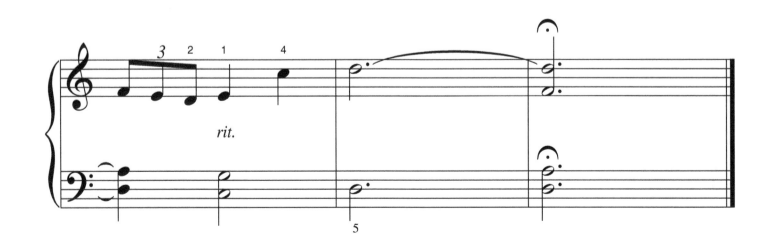

CANTINA BAND

from STAR WARS: EPISODE IV - A NEW HOPE

Music by
JOHN WILLIAMS

DUEL OF THE FATES

from STAR WARS: EPISODE I - THE PHANTOM MENACE

Music by
JOHN WILLIAMS

Majestically

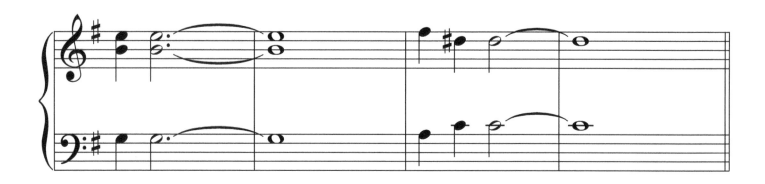

Quickly

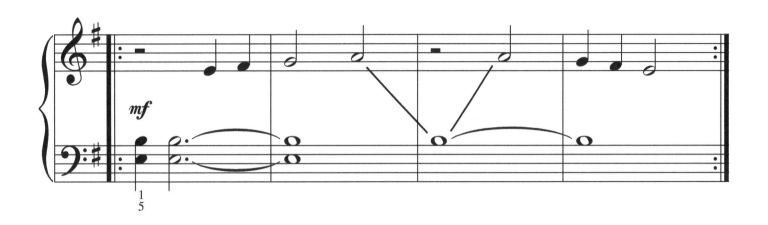

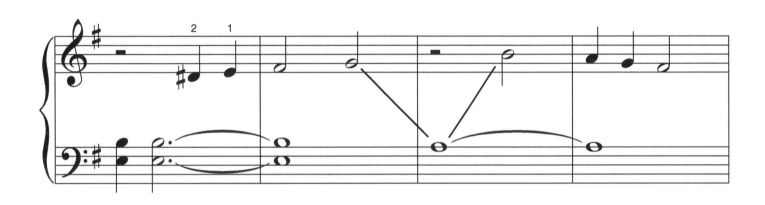

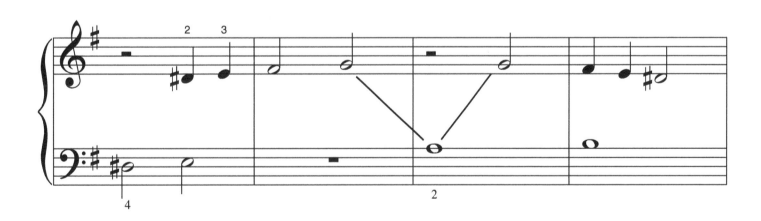

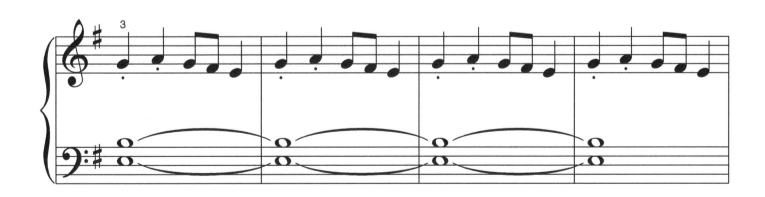

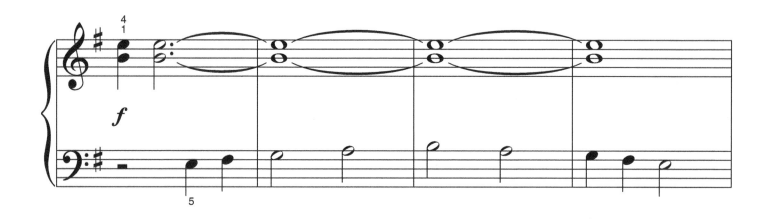

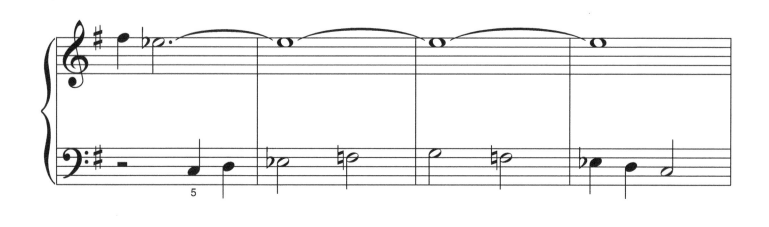

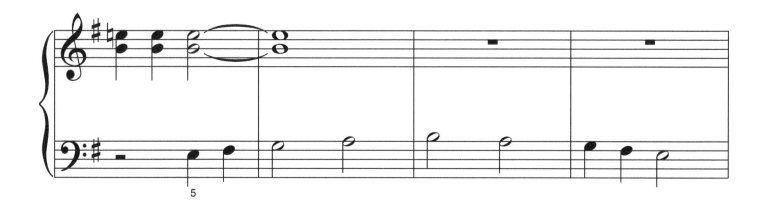

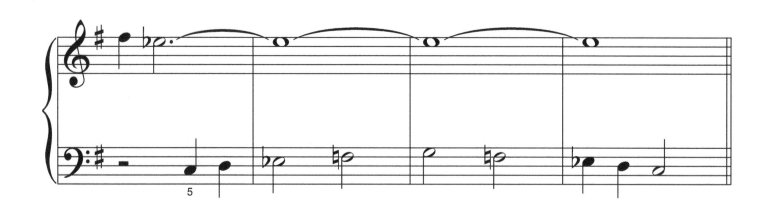

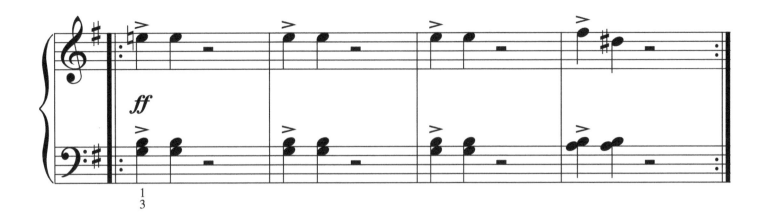

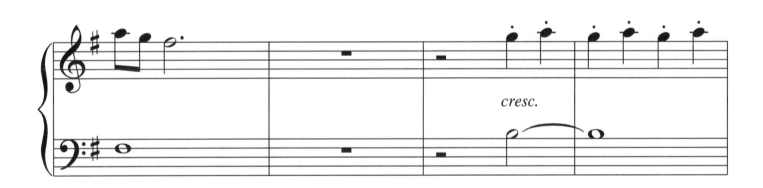

THE IMPERIAL MARCH
(Darth Vader's Theme)
from THE EMPIRE STRIKES BACK - A Twentieth Century-Fox Release

Music by
JOHN WILLIAMS

Angrily

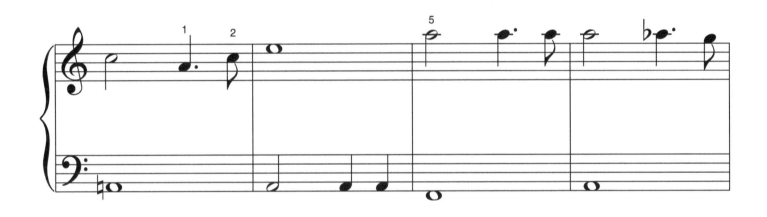

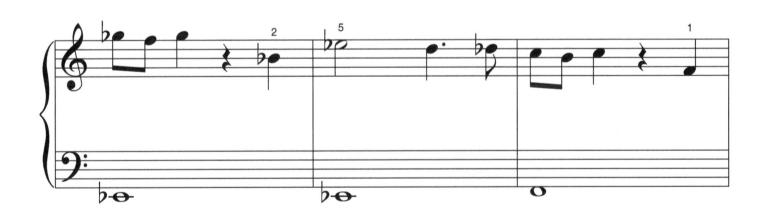

LUKE AND LEIA

from STAR WARS: EPISODE VI - RETURN OF THE JEDI

Music by
JOHN WILLIAMS

Slowly

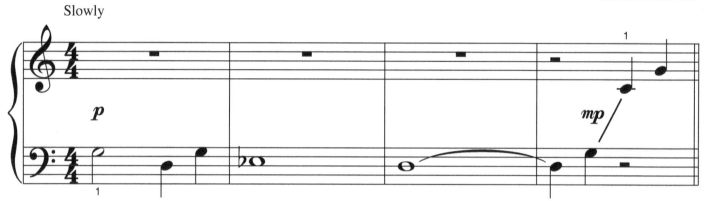

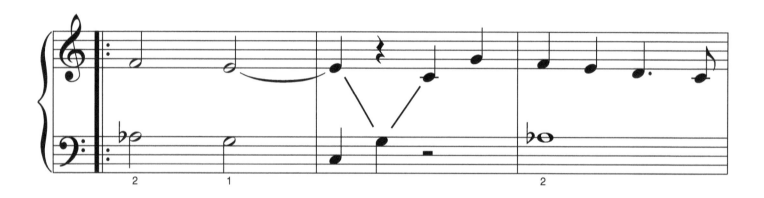

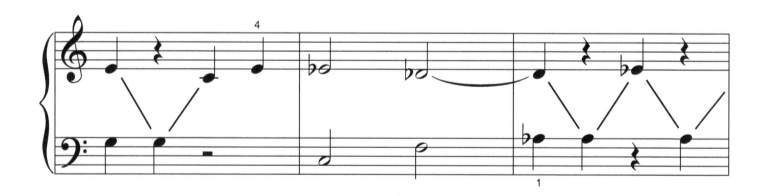

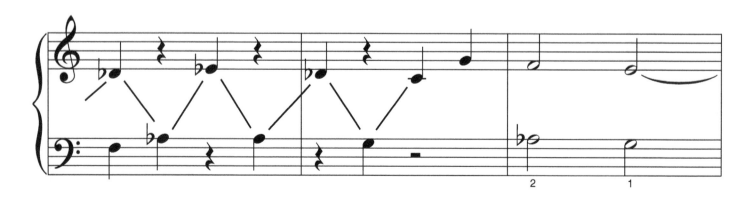

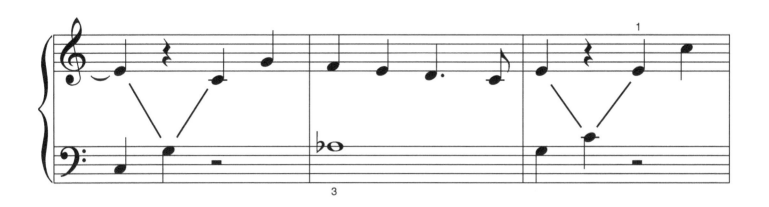

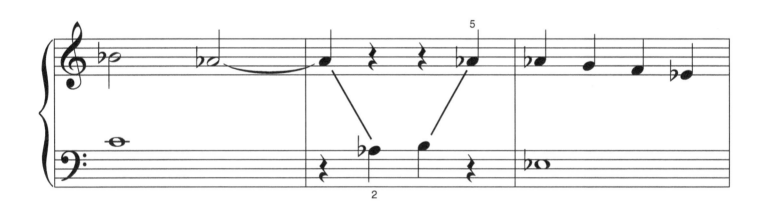

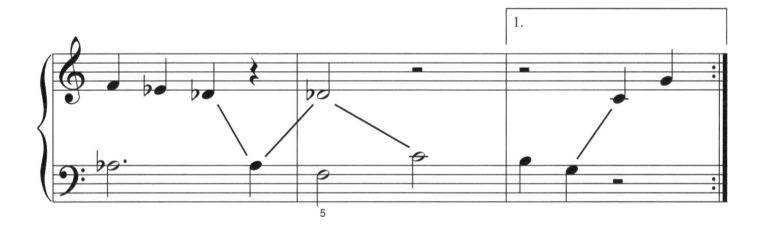

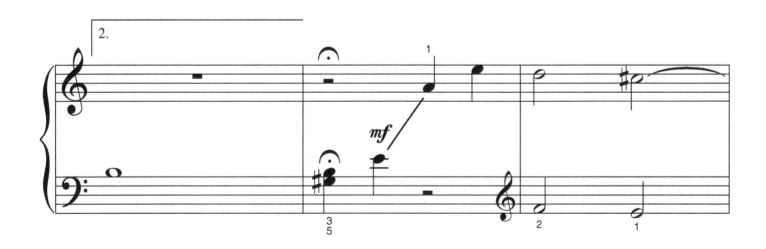

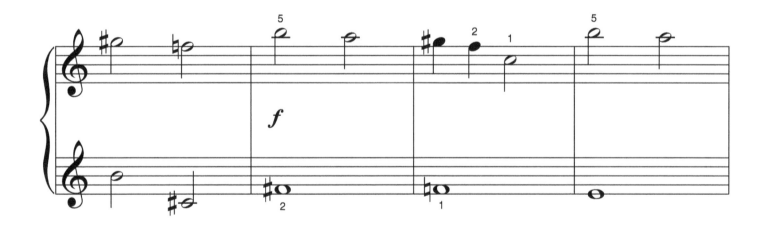

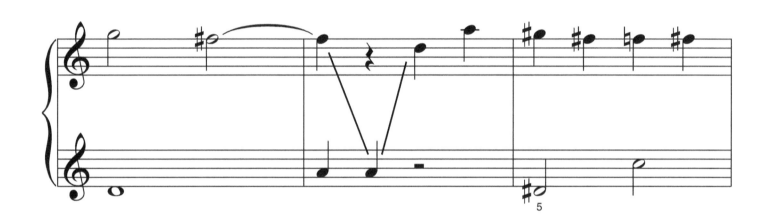

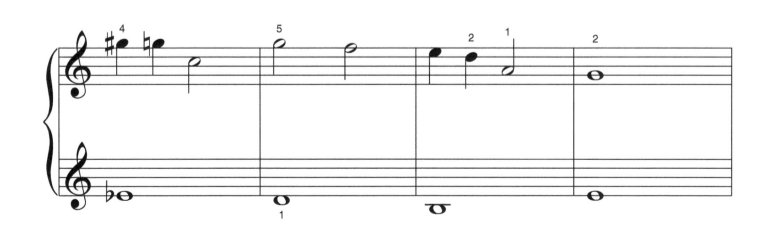

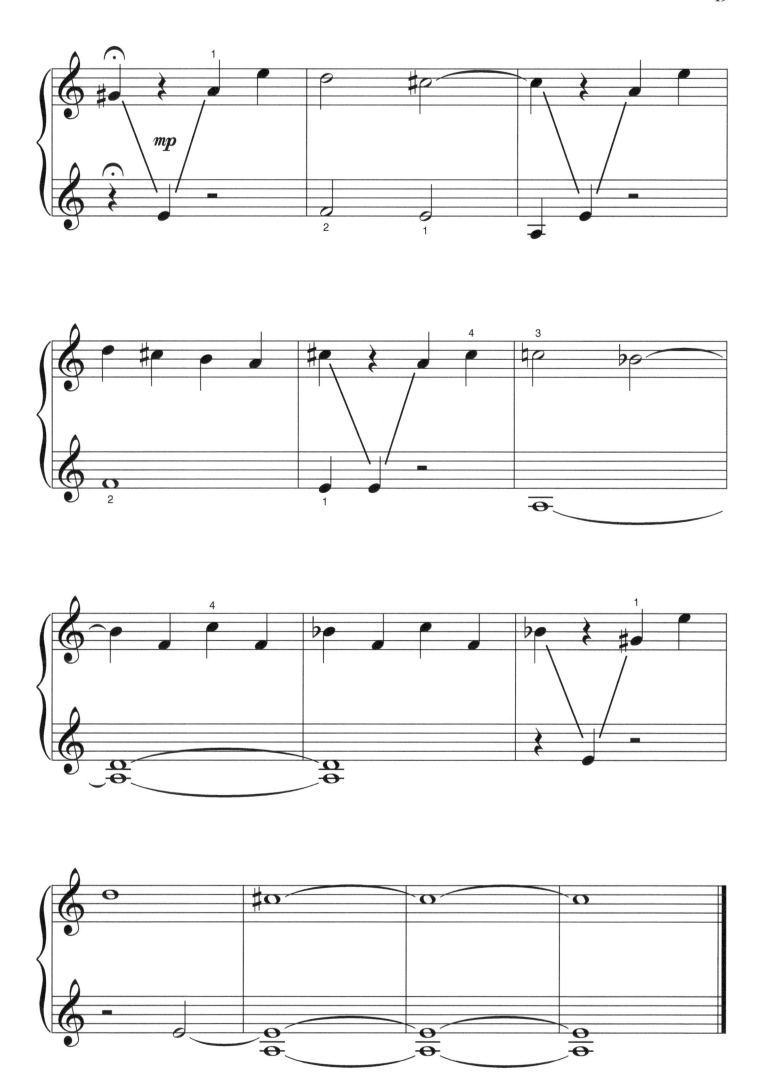

PRINCESS LEIA'S THEME

from STAR WARS - A Twentieth Century-Fox Release

Music by
JOHN WILLIAMS

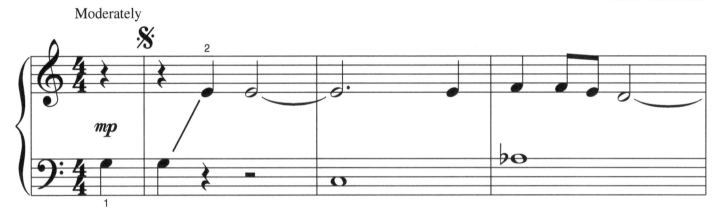

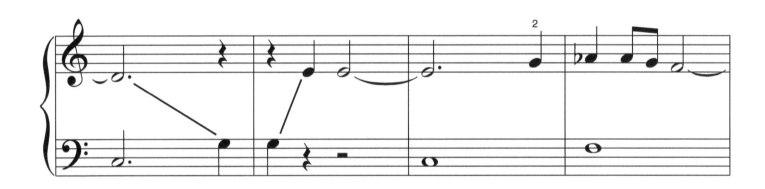

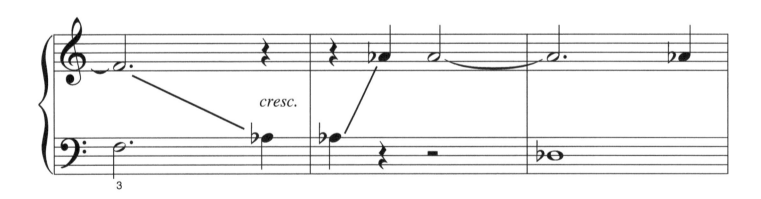

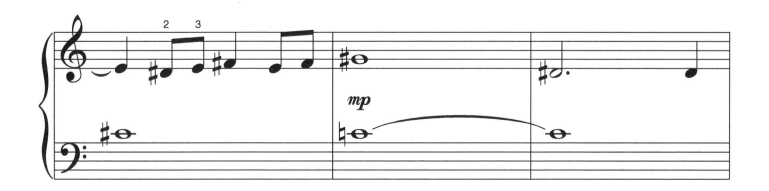

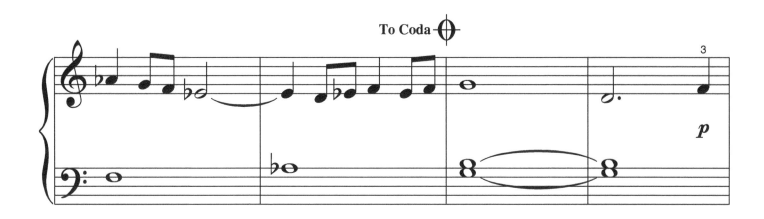

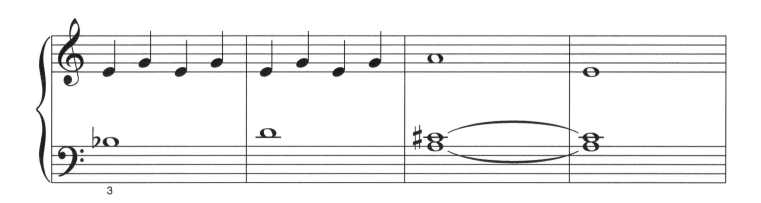

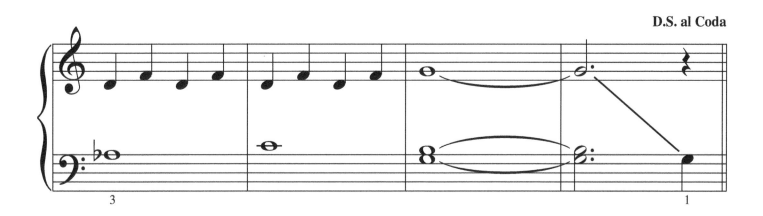

CODA

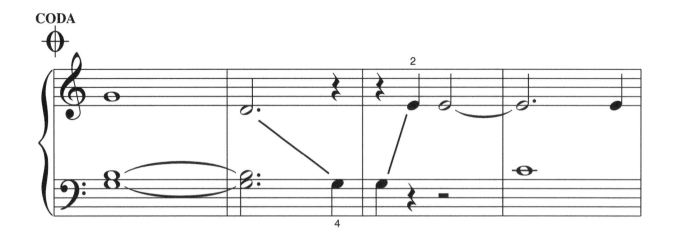

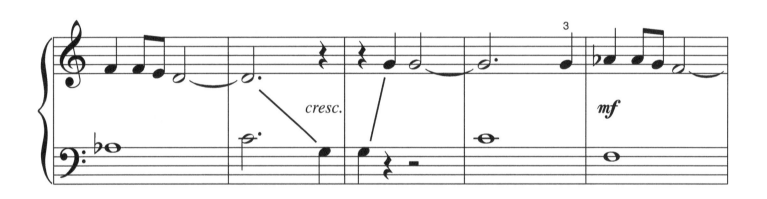

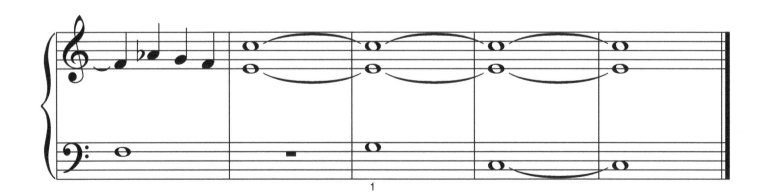

MAY THE FORCE BE WITH YOU

Music by
JOHN WILLIAMS

Slowly

mp

With pedal

STAR WARS
(Main Theme)
from STAR WARS, THE EMPIRE STRIKES BACK
and RETURN OF THE JEDI - Twentieth Century-Fox Releases

Music by
JOHN WILLIAMS

Majestically

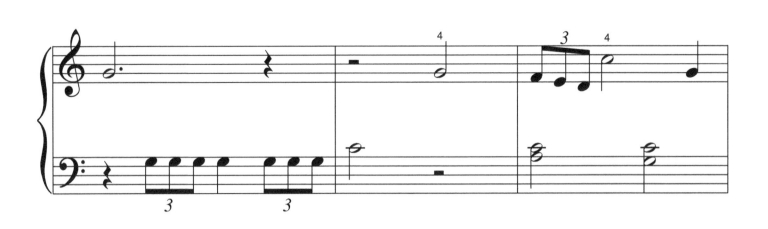

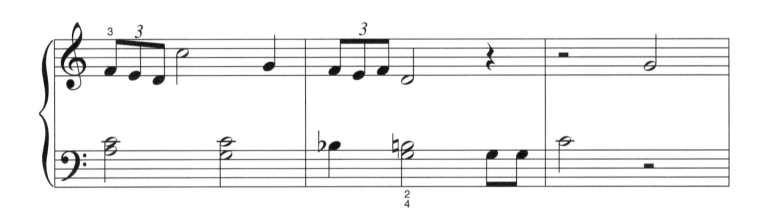

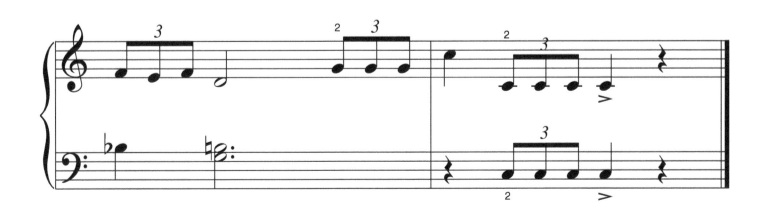

THE THRONE ROOM
(And End Title)
from STAR WARS: EPISODE IV - A NEW HOPE

Music by
JOHN WILLIAMS

Majestically

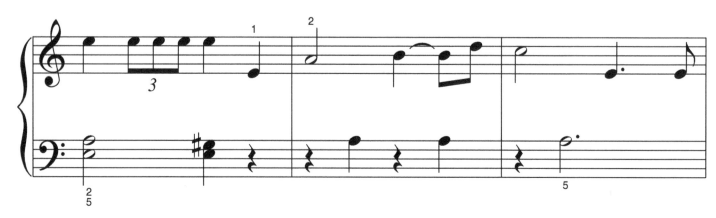

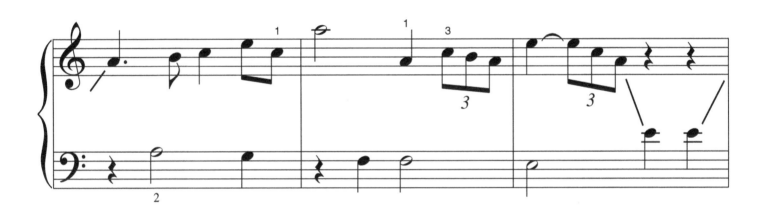

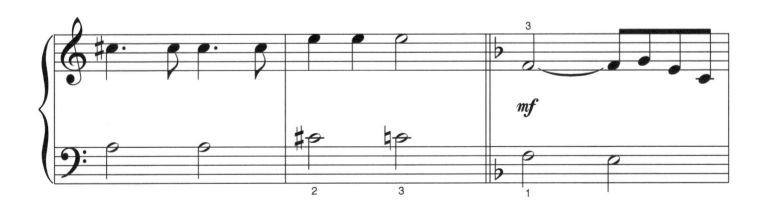

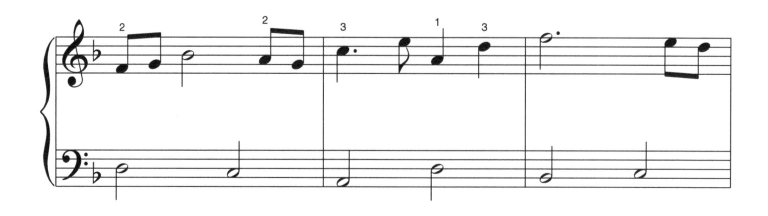

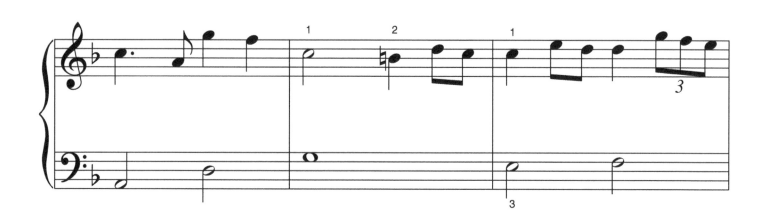

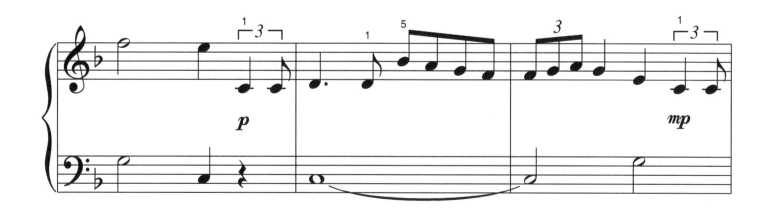

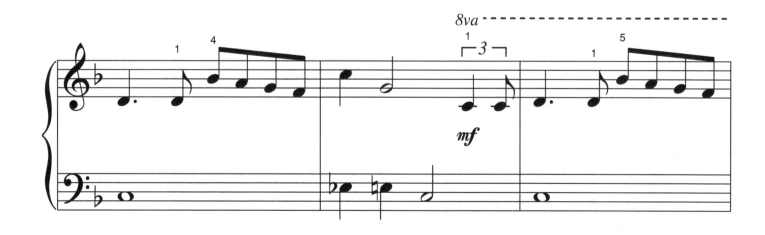

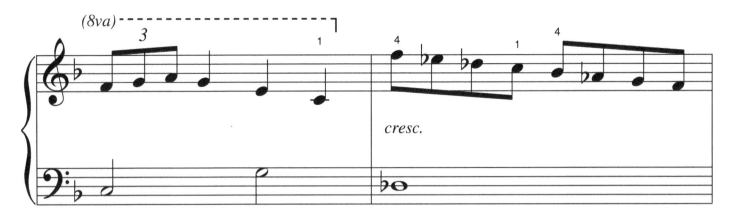

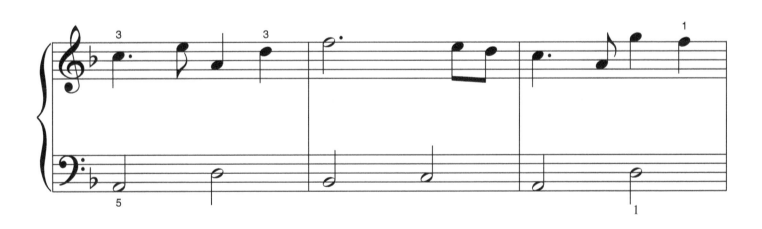

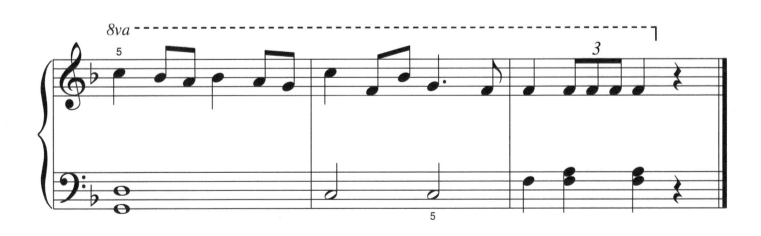

YODA'S THEME

from THE EMPIRE STRIKES BACK - A Twentieth Century-Fox Release

Music by
JOHN WILLIAMS

Slowly

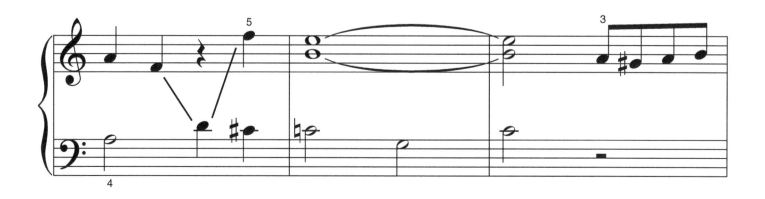

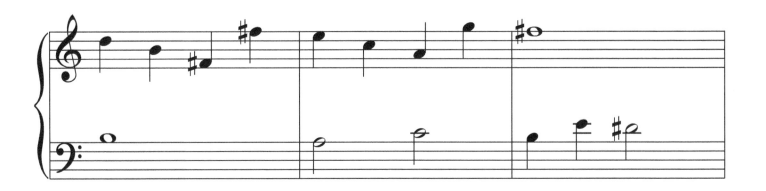

A little faster

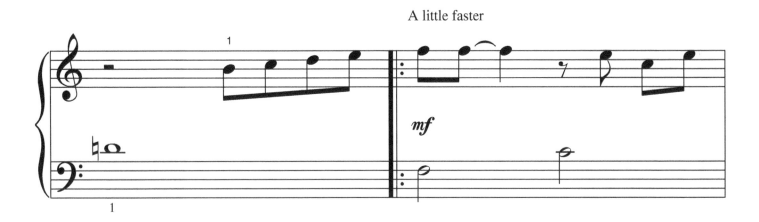

Tempo I

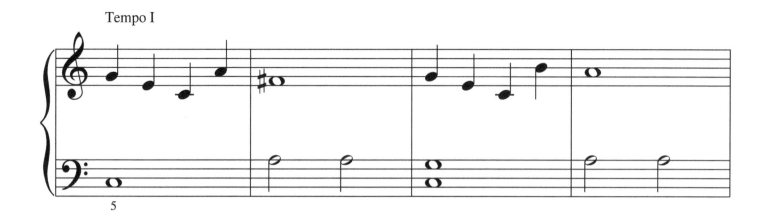

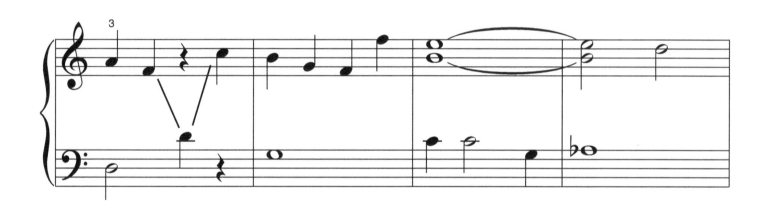

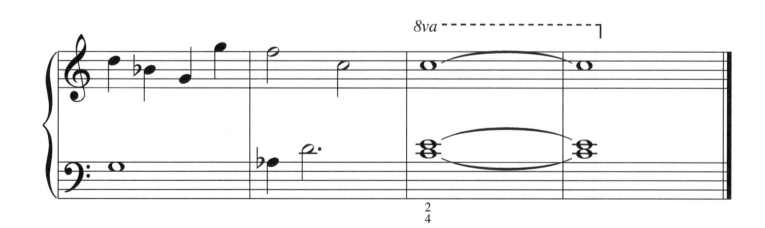